RECYCLEDscience

BRING OUT YOUR SCIENCE GENIUS WITH SODA BOTTLES, POTATO CHIP BAGS, AND MORE UNEXPECTED STUFF

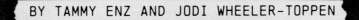

BY TAMMY ENZ AND JODI WHEELER-TOPPEN

Capstone Young Readers
a capstone imprint

TABLE OF CONTENTS

CHAPTER ONE

AWESOME CRAFT STICK SCIENCE

STICK AROUND!

There's nothing like a tasty snack on a stick. But when you finish smacking that snack, don't discard the stick. Repurpose it! Do more than repurpose it. Reveal science at work with awesome craft stick science projects. Their unique shape and material properties make them ideal for science projects. So eat up. Then gather some tools and get to work! (Don't forget that jumbo craft sticks make awesome projects too.)

HAPPY ACCIDENT

More than 2 billion Popsicles are sold each year. But did you know their invention was accidental? Eleven-year-old Frank Epperson discovered the treat in 1905. He left his sugary drink with a stir stick outside overnight. After a chilly night, he found his drink frozen into a Popsicle.

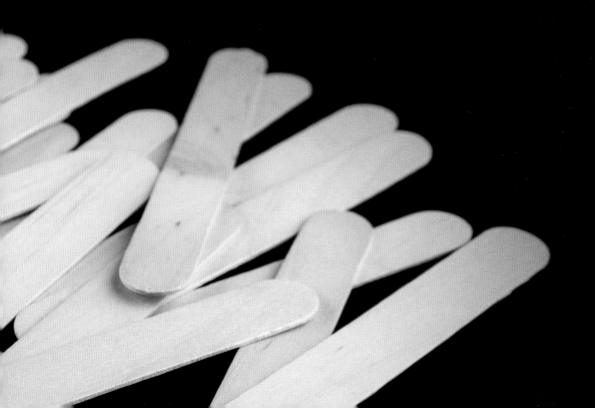

WOODEN CHAIN

Did you ever wonder how curved wooden furniture is made? Usually bending a wood craft stick causes it to snap. But you can unlock the secret to bending wood with this experiment.

BRANCH OF SCIENCE: BIOLOGY
CONCEPT: PROPERTIES OF WOOD

YOU'LL NEED:

- Slow cooker or crockpot
- Water
- 5 to 10 craft sticks
- Tongs
- 5 to 10 round cups or milk jug caps

SAFETY FIRST:

Have an adult help out when using a cooker.

PUT IT TOGETHER:

STEP 1: Fill the cooker half full of water. Place the craft sticks inside. Cook for one to two hours at medium heat.

STEP 2: Carefully remove a stick with tongs. Allow the stick to cool for about a minute before touching it. Slowly begin bending the stick into a circle.

STEP 3: Fit the circle inside a cup. Repeat with the other sticks and cups.

STEP 4: Leave the sticks inside the cups overnight. Remove them, and carefully fit the links together to form a chain.

STEP 3   STEP 4

REUSABLE KNOWLEDGE:

Wood is a hygroscopic material. It can absorb water from its environment. The cells that make up wood have cellulose in their walls. Cellulose gives wood its strength. Dry wood is strong but brittle. Water makes cellulose soft and stretchable.

STRUCTURE OF WOOD

Live trees contain lots of water. Up to two-thirds of a tree's weight comes from the water inside of it. The water keeps the cell walls soft, allowing the tree to bend and sway without breaking.

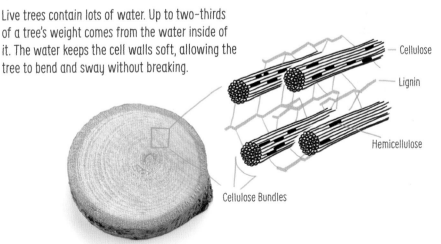

Cellulose

Lignin

Hemicellulose

Cellulose Bundles

CRYSTAL SNOWFLAKE

This chemistry experiment appears almost magical. Sparkling crystals appear overnight from clear liquid. Give it a try!

BRANCH OF SCIENCE: **CHEMISTRY**
CONCEPT: **SUPER SATURATED SOLUTION**

YOU'LL NEED:

- Pipe cleaner (any color)
- Scissors
- 6-inch-(15-centimeter-) long piece of string
- Craft stick
- Large drinking glass or jar
- 1.5 cups (.35 liter) boiling water
- 3 tablespoons (45 grams) of borax
- Spoon

SAFETY FIRST:
Have an adult help out when using hot water.

PUT IT TOGETHER:

STEP 1: Cut the pipe cleaner into three equal length sections. Twist the pieces together at their centers. Spread out the pieces to form a six-pointed asterisk.

STEP 2: Tie one end of the string around one arm of the asterisk. Tie the other end around the center of the craft stick.

STEP 3: Lay the craft stick across the top of the glass, hanging the asterisk inside the jar. Adjust the string so the asterisk hangs about halfway down the jar.

STEP 4: Remove the asterisk, and pour the boiling water into the jar. Slowly stir in the borax powder.

STEP 5: Replace the asterisk inside the jar. Place the project somewhere it won't be disturbed. Leave it alone overnight, and observe it in the morning.

STEP 1

STEP 2

STEP 3

REUSABLE KNOWLEDGE:

In this experiment you created a super saturated liquid. By heating the water, you added energy. The energy caused water molecules to speed up. They collided with borax crystals, dissolving them. Hot water dissolves more crystals than cold water. So when the water cooled, the borax crystals returned to their solid form. The pipe cleaner was an easy place for the crystals to cling.

WHAT IS BORAX?

Borax is a natural mineral that dissolves easily in water. It is found in dry lake beds and has many uses. In ancient times it was used for preserving food and mummies. Ancient Chinese pottery makers used it in glazes. Today it is used in detergent and cleaning products. It is also used as a fire retardant and tooth whitener.

CHAIN REACTION

Do you like lining up dominoes just to watch them fall in a chain reaction? Then you'll love this experiment. It takes a little patience and help from a friend. But it creates lots of fun and a lesson in physics.

BRANCH OF SCIENCE: PHYSICS
CONCEPT: POTENTIAL AND KINETIC ENERGY

YOU'LL NEED:

- A pile of craft sticks (jumbo ones work best)
- A friend

SAFETY FIRST:

Wear eye protection when working on this project.

PUT IT TOGETHER:

STEP 1: Take four sticks and lay them on a flat surface in a square shape. Overlap their ends by about 2 inches (5 cm). Make sure one end of each stick is lapped under while its other end is lapped over adjacent sticks.

STEP 2: Slide the ends of the two sticks closest to you so their ends overlap forming a "V." Hold your thumb on the tip of the V and keep it there.

STEP 3: Have a friend weave another stick over and under the sticks on your left side. If done correctly, the sticks will be difficult to weave, but will hold together.

STEP 4: Now have your friend do the same thing to the stick ends on your right.

STEP 5: Alternate back and forth from side to side. Weave the tips of the two outermost sticks.

STEP 6: When you run out of sticks, count down. Let both ends of the weave go at the same time. Watch out!

STEP 3

REUSABLE KNOWLEDGE:

Most materials bounce back when bent. (Although if bent too far they'll snap.) The energy in these bent sticks is called potential energy. This energy is stored up, waiting to return the sticks to their normal shape. When you finally let go, the stored energy turns into movement. This moving energy is called kinetic energy.

BOW AND ARROW

This bow and arrow project is a ton of fun to build. It's even more fun to play with. Test out a physics fact, and have a blast at the same time!

BRANCH OF SCIENCE: PHYSICS
CONCEPT: ACCELERATION DUE TO GRAVITY

YOU'LL NEED:

- 12 craft sticks
- Ruler
- 2 pencils (1 sharpened and 1 unsharpened)
- Hot glue gun
- 3 corks
- Utility knife
- Rubber band
- 2 twist ties
- Unsharpened pencil
- A friend
- Timer

SAFETY FIRST:
Have an adult help out when using hot glue and sharp tools such as a utility knife.

PUT IT TOGETHER:

STEP 1: Measure and mark with a pencil the center of each of the craft sticks.

STEP 2: Overlap the ends of two sticks to form a 120-degree angle. Hot glue them together.

STEP 3: Glue another stick to the end of one of these sticks at the same angle. You will form a bow shape.

STEP 4: Glue the ends of another stick to connect the center of one angled piece to the center of the middle piece.

STEP 5: Repeat Step 4 to connect the other angled piece to the middle piece.

STEP 6: Glue the ends of a sixth stick to connect the centers of the pieces added in steps 4 and 5.

STEP 7: Repeat steps 2-6 to make another bow shape.

STEP 8: Use the utility knife to cut a cork in half to make two shorter corks.

STEP 9: Repeat Step 8 with the other two corks.

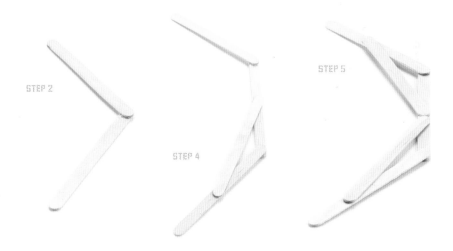

STEP 2

STEP 4

STEP 5

STEP 10: Sandwich five of the cork pieces between the bows. Glue them at the bow ends, at the angles, and in the center of the straight piece.

STEP 11: Stretch the rubber band between the bow ends. Connect each end of the rubber band to a cork with a twist tie.

STEP 12: To make the arrow, have an adult help you use the utility knife to cut a slit down the center of the unsharpened end of the pencil wide enough for the rubber band to fit into.

STEP 13: Make a horizontal pencil mark on a wall at about your shoulder height.

STEP 14: Rest the pencil on the center cork. Slide the slit over the rubber band.

STEP 15: Pull back the pencil. Release it perfectly horizontally, even with the mark on the wall. Have your friend time how long it takes to hit the ground.

STEP 16: Now have your friend time how long it takes for a pencil to hit the ground when you simply drop it from the height of the mark on the wall. How do the times compare?

REUSABLE KNOWLEDGE:

Both pencils should hit the ground at nearly the same time. Why? The answer is gravity. One pencil moves horizontally and the other straight down. But gravity pulls both downward at the same rate.

SAFETY FIRST:

Don't release your arrow in the direction of people.

HARMONICA

Do you like to make music, or at least really cool sounds? Try your hand at this project. It will give you more than a tune to play. It will give you a sense of how sound waves work.

BRANCH OF SCIENCE: PHYSICS
CONCEPT: SOUND WAVES/PITCH

YOU'LL NEED:

- 2 jumbo craft sticks
- Waxed paper
- Pen
- Scissors
- 2 rubber bands
- 2 wooden toothpicks

PUT IT TOGETHER:

STEP 1: Trace a craft stick onto the waxed paper with the pen. Cut out the shape. Repeat to make another piece.

STEP 2: Sandwich the waxed paper pieces between the sticks. Wrap rubber bands tightly about 0.5 inch (1 cm) from each end of the sticks.

STEP 3: Carefully insert the toothpicks between the waxed paper sheets. Slide one in each end, next to the rubber band.

STEP 4: Place the flat side of the harmonica between your lips. Blow gently in the center.

STEP 5: To change the sound, move the sticks farther from and then closer to the rubber bands.

STEP 1

STEP 3

REUSABLE KNOWLEDGE:

Sound is caused by vibrations. People's vocal cords vibrate to make sounds. Parts of musical instruments also vibrate. The sound in this harmonica comes from vibrating waxed paper. The number of times that a sound wave vibrates in a certain period of time is its frequency. High-pitched sounds have high frequencies. Moving the toothpicks closer causes the paper to vibrate quicker. It creates a higher pitch.

Sound travels through the air at about 1,126 feet (343 meters) per second. It travels even faster in water. Sound must travel through a medium such as gas (air), water, or a solid object. Because there is no air on the moon, astronauts cannot hear each other talk there. They must use a radio.

PADDLEBOAT

Have you ever watched paddleboats churning through the water? This project will give you a look at how they work. Better yet, it will give you a look at how many things move. Newton's Third Law of Motion describes how boats, birds, and even rockets move.

BRANCH OF SCIENCE: **PHYSICS**
CONCEPT: **NEWTON'S THIRD LAW OF MOTION**

YOU'LL NEED:

- Piece of wood about 2 inches (5 cm) wide x 4 inches (10 cm) long x 0.75-inch (2-cm) thick
- 2 jumbo craft sticks
- 3 rubber bands
- Hot glue gun
- Piece of plastic cut from a milk jug 1.5-inch (4-cm) square
- Pool or tub of water

SAFETY FIRST:

Have an adult help out when using hot glue.

PUT IT TOGETHER:

STEP 1: Place the flat sides of the craft sticks along the long sides of the block of wood. Allow their ends to stick about halfway past the end of the wood block.

STEP 2: Use two rubber bands to hold the sticks to the block of wood.

STEP 3: Place the third rubber band around the free ends of the sticks, 1 inch (2.5 cm) from their ends. Hot glue the rubber band to the outside faces of the sticks.

STEP 4: Place the plastic piece in the center of this rubber band. Holding the boat upright, wind the plastic several turns toward the back of the paddleboat.

STEP 5: Place the boat in water, and release the paddle.

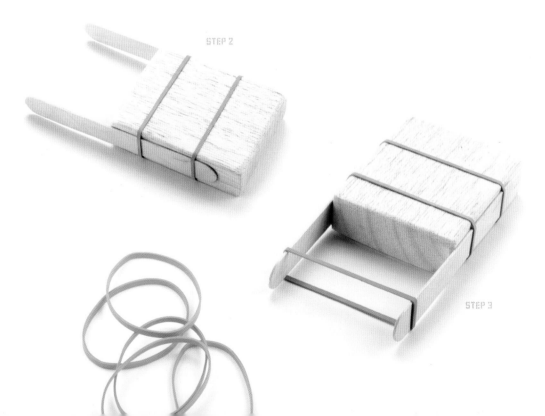

STEP 2

STEP 3

REUSABLE KNOWLEDGE:

When the paddle hits the water's surface it pushes water back. This causes the boat to move forward. This experiment shows Newton's Third Law of Motion. This law states that for every action there is an equal and opposite reaction. Newton's Third Law of Motion applies to all kinds of motion. What happens if you hit a brick wall with your fist? The wall doesn't move backward due to your forward action. But it does push your fist back with the same force you exerted. You feel the force as a great big "ouch!"

SIR ISAAC NEWTON (1643–1727)

Newton was a great scientist from the 1600s and 1700s. He is famous for his study of gravity. His three laws of motion form the basis for modern physics.

NEWTON'S LAWS

1. An object at rest stays at rest. A moving object will keep moving unless acted on. (Law of inertia)

2. Acceleration is produced when a force acts on a mass. Heavy objects take more force to move the same distance.

3. For every action there is an equal and opposite reaction.

HELICOPTER

Test this project outside or in a room with high ceilings. Your helicopter sails high, giving you a peek at the science behind helicopter propellers.

BRANCH OF SCIENCE: PHYSICS
CONCEPT: LIFT VERSUS GRAVITY

YOU'LL NEED:

- Pan of boiling water
- Craft stick
- Tongs
- Heavy books
- Wooden skewer
- Sandpaper
- Hot glue gun
- 18 –nch (46-cm) piece of string
- Empty thread spool

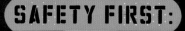

SAFETY FIRST:

Have an adult help out when using hot water and hot glue.

PUT IT TOGETHER:

STEP 1: Place the stick in the boiling water for about 10 minutes. With the tongs, pull out the stick, and hold it for a few seconds while it cools.

STEP 2: Twist the ends in opposite directions. Place one end between upright books. Set heavy books on the other end to hold the twist in the stick. Allow the stick to dry for several hours.

STEP 3: Snap the skewer in half. You will only need half. Use the sandpaper to make the broken end of one half smooth and flat.

STEP 4: Use the hot glue to glue the flat end of the skewer piece to the center of the twisted craft stick.

STEP 5: Wrap the string around the skewer about 2 inches (5 cm) from its pointed end. Place this end into the center of the spool.

STEP 6: Holding the spool, grab the loose end of the string and pull it to launch the helicopter. (Now wind the string in the opposite direction. Does the winding direction make a difference in how it flies?)

STEP 2

STEP 5

REUSABLE KNOWLEDGE:

Angled propellers move air faster across their tops than their bottoms. This creates suction, causing the propeller to lift. Spinning fast creates enough lift to overcome gravity.

FAST FACT:

Helicopters have one propeller on top and one on their tail. Why? The tail prop keeps the helicopter stable. Otherwise the helicopter would spin with the rotations of the main propeller.

CORK LAUNCHER

Build a rubber band launcher to bring some fun and excitement to your day! A rubber band's ability to stretch and spring gives this launcher its gusto. Whip up this project, and see the science behind a rubber band's power.

BRANCH OF SCIENCE: CHEMISTRY
CONCEPT: PROPERTIES OF ELASTOMERS

YOU'LL NEED:

- 4 jumbo craft sticks
- Hot glue gun
- 2 corks
- Utility knife
- Wooden clothespin
- 2 rubber bands

SAFETY FIRST:

Have an adult help out when using hot glue and sharp tools such as a utility knife. And never point your launcher at people or animals.

PUT IT TOGETHER:

STEP 1: Overlap the ends of two sticks by about 1 inch (2.5 cm). Hot glue them to make a longer stick. Repeat with the remaining two sticks.

STEP 2: Use the utility knife to slice one of the corks in half. You'll have two shorter corks.

STEP 3: Sandwich one of the cork halves between the ends of the sticks from Step 1. Sandwich the uncut cork between their other ends. Glue the corks in place.

STEP 4: Place the launcher on one of its flat sides. Glue a flat side of the clothespin near the end with the uncut cork. Its legs should face up the slope.

STEP 5: Loop one end of a rubber band through the other. Tuck it inside its other end to form a knot. This will connect the rubber bands.

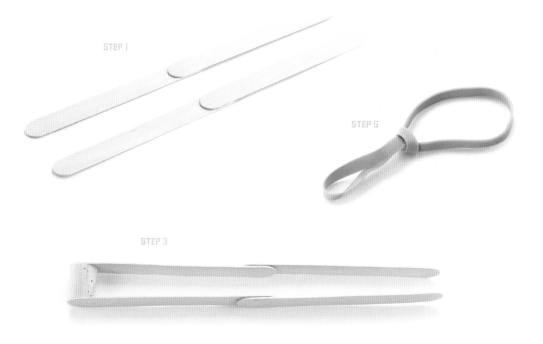

STEP 1

STEP 5

STEP 3

STEP 6: Wrap one of the rubber bands several times tightly around the end of the launcher opposite the clothespin. Leave the other rubber band trailing toward the clothespin.

STEP 7: Pull this rubber band back, and snap it into the mouth of the clothespin.

STEP 8: Place the remaining half cork near the mouth of the clothespin. Place it inside the rubber band loop.

STEP 9: To launch, press open the clothespin.

STEPS 7-9

REUSABLE KNOWLEDGE:

Rubber bands are elastomers. Elastomers are tangled chains of molecules that straighten when stretched. They can be stretched to twice their original length before snapping back. When stretching a rubber band, you add potential energy to it. The potential energy is stored to launch your cork.

ELASTOMERS

When stretching a rubber band, you untangle a chain of molecules.

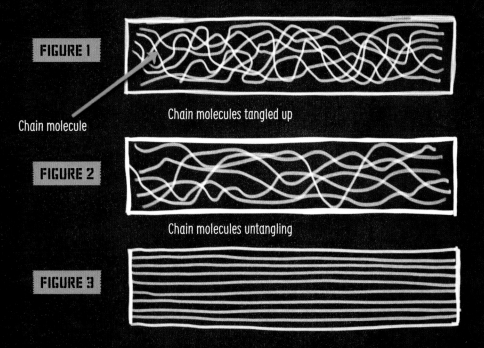

FIGURE 1

Chain molecule

Chain molecules tangled up

FIGURE 2

Chain molecules untangling

FIGURE 3

FAST FACT:

Rubber is harvested from the sap of rubber trees.

CHAPTER TWO
INCREDIBLE SNACK PACKET SCIENCE

IN THE BAG

Munching a bag of snacks or tube of chips makes for a tasty break. But have you ever stopped to think of the technological marvels behind snack bags and tubes? Have you ever wondered why many have silver insides? Maybe you've wondered if those bags and tubes could ever be used for something new. Well, pop open a snack, and eat up. Your questions are about to be answered. Sealed in these packages are all kinds of science. When repurposed, they shed light on some amazing scientific facts. Go on! Satisfy your hunger and your scientific curiosity.

BoPET

Nobody likes soggy potato chips. That's why a special kind of plastic is used for snack bags. Biaxially-oriented polyethylene terephthalate (BoPET) is finely stretched polyester lined with aluminum that makes chip bags tough. The layers also keep oily chips from leaking out. The aluminum layer keeps out oxygen that can make chips taste bad.

TIP:

To clean your snack bags and tubes before use, simply wipe away the oil with a paper towel. No soap is needed!

AMPLIFYING SPEAKER

Playing tunes on a smartphone or music player is great. But does your speaker let you down when you crank it up? Try amping up the sound with this project.

PUT IT TOGETHER:

STEP 1: Lay the binder clips facing each other with their tabs open. Place the center of the tube between them. Use hot glue to glue the clips in place.

STEP 2: Measure and make a mark on the top of the tube, 2 inches (5 cm) from the bottom end of the tube.

STEP 3: Use the utility knife to carefully cut a slit at this mark.

STEP 4: Using the width of your player as a guide, slowly widen the slit a little at a time. Widen the slit until you have a slot that your player will fit tightly into.

STEP 5: Loosely stuff the tissue into the open end of the tube. Make sure it doesn't bunch up.

STEP 5

STEP 6: Stick your player into the slot. Face the speaker toward the open end of the can. Sit back, and enjoy some amplified tunes!

REUSABLE KNOWLEDGE:

Music is caused by vibrations carried on sound waves. Waves travel through air in widening circles like ripples on water. The farther you are from a sound, the quieter it is. When you use this amp, the can captures sound waves before they spread out. The waves bounce off the can, causing an amplified sound. The tissue softens the sound to reduce echoes.

ARE YOU BEING "BUGGED" BY YOUR BAG?

If you're telling a secret, stay away from chip bags. Why? Somebody may be listening! Researchers at the Massachusetts Institute of Technology (MIT) use a special camera to capture bag vibrations. These vibrations, caused by sound waves, can be decoded into words.

JUMPING JACK

Would you like the power to command something to move without laying a finger on it? That power is all yours with this project. Amaze your friends with your invisible display of strength.

BRANCH OF SCIENCE: PHYSICS
CONCEPT: ELECTROSTATIC INDUCTION

YOU'LL NEED:

- Clean, dry snack bag
- Ruler
- Pen
- Scissors
- Tape
- Balloon

PUT IT TOGETHER:

STEP 1: Lay the bag flat. Draw the shape of half a person along one of the folded edges of the bag. Make the centerline of the person fall on the fold.

STEP 2: Cut out and unfold the pattern.

STEP 3: Lay the cutout on a table, silver side down. Tape the tips of its feet to the table.

STEP 4: Fold the cutout over so the silver side is up. Make sure the cutout still rests on the table.

STEP 5: Blow up the balloon and tie it. Hold the balloon near the cutout. What happens?

STEP 6: Rub the balloon quickly back and forth on your hair for about 10 seconds.

STEP 7: Hold the balloon over the person. Now watch "Jack" jump to grab it.

STEP 1

STEP 4

REUSABLE KNOWLEDGE:

Normally the charges in a balloon are balanced. However, when rubbing the balloon on your hair, electrons transfer. The balloon becomes negatively charged by static electricity. When held near the cutout, the balloon realigns the charges in the metal. The metal's positive charges move toward the negatively charged balloon. This realignment is called induction. So why does your hair reach out toward the balloon after rubbing it? You've given your hair a positive charge. Opposite charges attract, so your hair is attracted to the balloon.

UNDERWATER SPYGLASS

Looking for underwater treasure could be a lot of fun. But underwater snooping is blurry business. Pull your head out of the water. Pull out your spyglass, and clear up your water view.

BRANCH OF SCIENCE: PHYSICS
CONCEPT: OPTICAL REFRACTION

YOU'LL NEED:

- Clean, dry potato chip tube with a clear lid
- Can opener
- Hot glue gun

SAFETY FIRST:
Have an adult help out when using hot glue, and get an adult's permission to use your spyglass in water.

PUT IT TOGETHER:

STEP 1: Use the can opener to remove the metal end of the tube.

STEP 2: Glue the lid on the other end of the can. Start by putting a bead of glue along the inside rim of the lid. Quickly put the lid on and hold it in place.

STEP 3: On the outside of the tube, place a bead of glue around the lid seam. This step makes the spyglass waterproof.

STEP 4: Take the spyglass to the lake or pool. First stick your face underwater to try to see objects beneath. What do they look like?

STEP 5: Now place the lidded end of the spyglass into the water and look into the open end. How do the objects appear now?

STEP 3

STEP 1

REUSABLE KNOWLEDGE:

As your eye absorbs light rays, it bends the rays in order to focus the image. This bending is called refraction. But water bends light rays too. When you look underwater without the spyglass, you see bent light. Your eyes can't focus this bent light. The spyglass inserts a cushion of air to help your eyes refract correctly.

PINHOLE CAMERA

If used with film, this pinhole camera could make an image like a real camera. Both work similarly. Without film, you can still see a wacky image and learn how cameras and the human eye work.

BRANCH OF SCIENCE: BIOLOGY
CONCEPT: OPTICAL INVERSION

YOU'LL NEED:

- Clean, dry potato chip tube with lid
- Ruler
- Pen
- Utility knife
- Pushpin
- Waxed paper
- Scissors
- Packing tape
- Sheet of aluminum foil, about 20 inches (51 cm) long

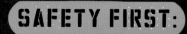

SAFETY FIRST:

Have an adult help out when using sharp tools such as a utility knife.

PUT IT TOGETHER:

STEP 1: Measure and mark with the pen a line 2 inches (5 cm) from the bottom of the tube all around the tube.

STEP 2: Carefully cut along this line with the utility knife. You will have two sections of the tube.

STEP 3: Turn the short section of tube over. Use the pushpin to make a small hole in the center of the metal end.

STEP 4: Use a pen to trace the lid on a sheet of waxed paper. Cut out this circle, and place it inside the lid.

STEP 5: Place the lid and waxed paper circle on the open end of the short section. Place the longer section on top of the lid. Tape the pieces together.

STEP 3

STEP 2

STEP 6: Tape one end of the foil sheet to the side of the tube. Roll the foil around the tube twice. Tape it in place.

STEP 7: Wrap the foil ends over or into the tube ends.

STEP 8: Take the camera outside on a sunny day. Closing one eye, look into the open end. What do you see? Raise your hand up and down in front of the pinhole. What happens?

STEP 6

STEP 7

REUSABLE KNOWLEDGE:

Like your eye, this camera captures images upside down. Your eye sends its upside down images to your brain. Your brain automatically turns the image upright. Since the chip canister doesn't have a brain, the image remains upside down!

Your eye gathers an image through its lens and focuses it on your retina. The image is projected upside down.

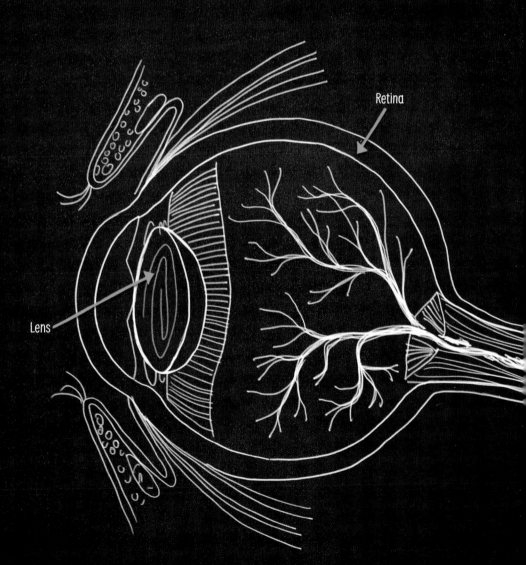

Retina

Lens

ICE CREAM MAKER

Is there a better snack than chips? You bet. How about ice cream? Finish up your chips. Then use the tube to create an ice cream maker. When you do you'll learn the scientific secret behind great ice cream.

BRANCH OF SCIENCE: CHEMISTRY
CONCEPT: MELTING POINT DEPRESSION

YOU'LL NEED:

- 4 cups (1 liter) of ice cubes
- 6 tablespoons rock or kosher salt
- Mixing bowl
- Spoon
- 0.5 cup (.125 liter) milk
- 1 tablespoon sugar
- 0.25 teaspoon vanilla extract
- Towel or oven mitts

PUT IT TOGETHER:

STEP 1: Stir the ice and salt together in the bowl with the spoon. Set the bowl aside.

STEP 2: Place the milk, sugar, and vanilla in the zipper bag. Close it tightly, sealing out most of the air. Gently shake the bag to mix the ingredients.

STEP 3: Spoon ice cubes from Step 1 into the chip tube. Fill it about one quarter full.

STEP 4: Drop the zipper bag into the tube.

STEP 2

STEP 3

STEP 4

STEP 5: Carefully spoon in ice on all sides of the bag.

STEP 6: Fill the rest of the tube with ice, and put on the lid.

STEP 7: Using the towel or oven mitts to hold the canister, shake the tube.

STEP 8: Every two minutes, check the ice. If there is room, add more ice.

STEP 9: Continue shaking for a total of six minutes.

STEP 10: Remove the lid, pull out the bag, and open it.
Enjoy your ice cream!

REUSABLE KNOWLEDGE:

To make great ice cream you need to whip the cream mixture while freezing it. Whipping it is easy to do by shaking the chip canister. Getting it cold enough is trickier. That's where the secret ingredient, salt, comes in. Salt lowers the temperature needed to melt ice. Now more heat energy is pulled from the ice cream to melt the ice. Thus the ice cream becomes colder faster.

Normally ice melts at 32 degrees Fahrenheit (0 degrees Celsius). Adding salt can lower its melting point to as low as -6.9 degrees F (-21.6 degrees C). Putting salt on roads during the winter months keeps the ice melted even at very cold temperatures.

STOMP ROCKET

A rocket project is always fun to make. This project relies on a snack bag's ability to hold in gas.

BRANCH OF SCIENCE: PHYSICS
CONCEPT: NEWTON'S SECOND LAW OF MOTION:
FORCE=MASS X ACCELERATION

YOU'LL NEED:

- Clean, dry snack bag
- Ruler
- Scissors
- Bendable straw
- Packing tape
- Paper towel
- Water

PUT IT TOGETHER:

STEP 1: Cut off the top 1 inch (2.5 cm) of the opened end of the bag.

STEP 2: Stick the longer end of the straw about 2 inches (5 cm) into the bag opening. Center it in the opening.

STEP 3: Tape the straw to the inside of the bag.

STEP 4: Tape the opening of the bag shut. Make sure to tape around the straw to make it airtight.

STEP 5: Reinforce the bottom seam of the bag with more tape.

STEP 6: Blow into the straw to fill the bag. Gently squeeze it to test for air leaks. Fix any leaks with tape.

STEP 7: Moisten the paper towel with the water, and tear off a small piece of the towel, enough to form into a pea-sized ball.

STEP 2

STEP 8

STEP 8: Blow up the bag using the straw. Stick the ball tightly into the end of the straw.

STEP 9: Place the bag on the ground. Stomp on it to see the ball fly!

REUSABLE KNOWLEDGE:

This experiment shows Newton's Second Law of Motion. This law states that acceleration is produced when a force acts on a mass. You applied a force when you stomped on the bag, releasing its air. The force you applied caused the ball to accelerate or speed up. Once the ball leaves the straw, gravity works to slow it down, pulling it to the ground.

EDIBLE RAFT

Want a good idea of how much gas is in bag of chips? Two South Korean college students found out in September 2014. They built a raft entirely from unopened potato chip bags. The 160 bags successfully carried them across the Han River in Seoul, South Korea.

Han River in Seoul, South Korea

SOLAR HOT DOG COOKER

Hot dogs and potato chips make great picnic food. You can have both with this project. Finish the chips. Then cook the dog. The best part is the sun does all the work.

SAFETY FIRST:

Have an adult help out when using hot glue and sharp tools such as a utility knife.

PUT IT TOGETHER:

STEP 1: Measure and make a mark 1 inch (2.5 cm) from each end of the tube. With the tube standing, set the ruler next to it as a straightedge to connect the marks. Draw a line to connect the marks.

STEP 2: Draw another line 3 inches (7.6 cm) from this line and parallel to it.

STEP 3: Connect the ends of the lines to make a rectangle.

STEP 4: Use the utility knife to cut out the rectangle. Save this piece for later.

STEP 5: With the lid on the tube, use the pushpin to make a hole in the lid's center.

STEP 6: Remove the lid, and place it over the metal end of the tube.

STEP 7: Using the lid as a guide, punch a hole into the metal's center with the nail and hammer.

STEP 8: Stick the skewer through the bottom of the can. Leave its point sticking slightly out of the top of the can.

STEP 9: To make the base for the cooker, remove the spring from the clothespin.

STEP 3

STEP 10: Place the clothespin halves flat side down. Place them parallel to each other 4 inches (10 cm) apart.

STEP 11: Put a dab of hot glue at the spots where the spring was connected. Set the cutout from Step 4 across the clothespin halves. This forms the base for the cooker.

STEP 12: Thread a hot dog onto the skewer. Replace the lid. Make sure the skewer pokes through the lid.

STEP 13: Lay the cooker on the base.

STEP 14: Place the plastic over the opening. Tape one of the long sides to the cooker.

STEP 15: Place the cooker in a sunny place. Rotate the cooker on the base so that the hot dog faces the sun.

STEP 16: Wait 15 to 30 minutes for the hot dog to cook. Lift the plastic flap to test if it is ready. Enjoy!

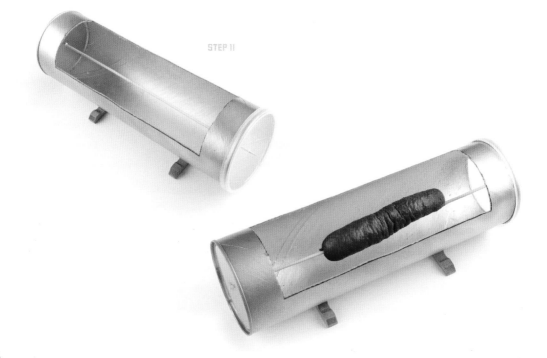

STEP 11

REUSABLE KNOWLEDGE:

The sun is a powerful energy source. On a sunny day, the sun supplies 100 watts of energy per 1 square foot (0.1 square meter). That's enough to light up a bright lightbulb. The secret to this project is capturing and focusing that power. The metallic curved shape of the cooker does just that.

HERO'S ENGINE

A couple thousand years ago, a mathematician and inventor called Hero of Alexandria created a unique engine. It propelled itself by shooting steam out of small holes. Using a chip can, you can make a similar machine. Yours will use water and the power of hydraulic head.

BRANCH OF SCIENCE: PHYSICS
CONCEPT: HYDRAULIC HEAD

YOU'LL NEED:

- Potato chip tube
- Ruler
- Pen
- Scissors
- 2 bendable drinking straws
- Hot glue gun
- 3 feet (1 meter) string
- Pitcher of water

SAFETY FIRST:

Have an adult help you when using hot glue.

PUT IT TOGETHER:

STEP 1: Measure and make a mark 1 inch (2.5 cm) from the bottom of the tube.

STEP 2: Using the tip of the scissors, punch a hole at this point. Twist the scissors point through the hole. Make it large enough to fit a drinking straw through.

STEP 3: Directly above this hole, make another mark 1 inch (2.5 cm) down from the top of the tube.

STEP 4: Make a small hole with the scissors point at this mark.

STEP 5: Repeat steps 1–4 on the opposite side of the can, directly across from the first holes.

STEP 6: Cut 4 inches (10 cm) from the non-bending end of both the straws. Discard these pieces.

STEP 7: Stick the longer end of one straw about 1 inch (2.5 cm) into one of the bottom holes. Glue it tightly in place.

STEP 7

STEP 4

STEP 10

STEP 8: Repeat Step 7 on the opposite side.

STEP 9: Bend the straws at right angles. Make them face opposite directions.

STEP 10: Thread the string through the upper holes. Pull it even on both sides.

STEP 11: Take the engine outside, and hang it from a tree branch or hook. Allow it lots of room to move.

STEP 12: Quickly pour water into the opening of the can to fill it. Jump back if you don't want to get wet!

REUSABLE KNOWLEDGE:

Notice how much faster the engine spins when the tube is full of water. It slows as the water level drops. Water is quite heavy. Therefore the deeper the water is, the more pressure it exerts. Shallow water exerts much less pressure. This phenomenon is called hydraulic head. When the hydraulic head in your engine is high, the pressure is greater. It shoots out water with a greater force, speeding up the engine. As the pressure decreases, so does the force propelling the engine.

A water tower works using a hydraulic head. Water is pumped up the tower where its weight pressurizes water pipes. The pressure pushes water out of your faucet. The tower must be higher than the houses it supplies.

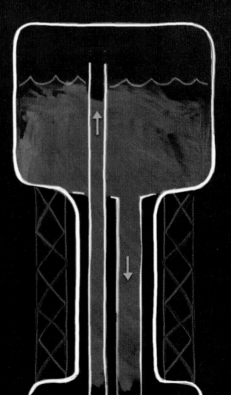

CHAPTER THREE

COOL PLASTIC BOTTLE SCIENCE

PLASTIC WITH PURPOSE

Milk, water, juice, pop—it seems like every drink comes in a plastic bottle. When you're done quenching your thirst, where do those bottles go? And where do they come from in the first place? Learn the answers to these questions and more. Then check out exciting ways to repurpose bottles and jugs into cool science experiments. Dig into your recycling bin, and get started.

GREAT PACIFIC GARBAGE PATCH

Plastic bottles are useful and durable. However, if not recycled they often end up in the Great Pacific Garbage Patch. Some scientists think this patch is twice the size of Texas. Trash makes its way into the ocean, where currents trap it in the waters of Asia and North America. Bottles can spend years floating in this garbage patch, breaking down into tiny pieces called microplastics. Sea animals often mistake plastic pieces for food. Eating plastic can kill them.

CLOUD IN A BOTTLE

Seeing a cloud in the sky might not seem remarkable. But there's a recipe for making clouds. Meet all the conditions, and you can whip one up in your kitchen!

BRANCH OF SCIENCE: EARTH SCIENCE
CONCEPT: CLOUD FORMATION

YOU'LL NEED:

- Clean 2-liter soda bottle with cap
- Water
- Dark sheet of construction paper
- Flashlight
- Matches
- A friend

PUT IT TOGETHER:

STEP 1: Fill the bottom of the bottle with about 1 inch (2.5 cm) of water. Screw on the cap. Shake the water around in the bottle.

STEP 2: Prop the paper against a wall. Set the bottle in front of it. Squeeze the bottle tightly. Let go.

STEP 3: As you let go, have a friend shine the flashlight into the bottle. Do you see a cloud?

STEP 1

STEP 4: Have an adult light two matches at the same time. Uncap the bottle, and drop the matches in the water. Quickly replace the cap.

STEP 5: Shake the bottle, and set it against the paper.

STEP 6: Squeeze the bottle tightly, and let it go while a friend shines light on the bottle. For a few seconds you will see a cloud appear.

STEP 7: Repeatedly squeeze the bottle to see the cloud form again and again.

REUSABLE KNOWLEDGE:

By shaking the bottle, you filled it with water vapor. Squeezing the bottle increased the air pressure and the temperature. Releasing the bottle decreased the air pressure and lowered the temperature. The cooling temperature caused water droplets to form and cling to the smoke. In the real world, water vapor clings to dust, smoke, or volcanic ash in the air to make clouds.

FAST FACT:

Bottles and many plastic packages are made from polyethylene terephthalate (PET). PET is a strong lightweight plastic. Its long chains of repeating molecules make it easy to form. Carbon dioxide can't seep through PET, making it ideal for soda bottles.

MILK JUG SIPHON

Think you can get water to flow uphill? How about keeping it flowing to drain a jug dry? You bet. It's easy to do and fun to watch again and again with this experiment.

BRANCH OF SCIENCE: EARTH SCIENCE
CONCEPT: ATMOSPHERIC PRESSURE

YOU'LL NEED:

- 2 clean milk jugs
- Water
- Food coloring (any color)
- 8–10 feet (2.4–3 m) clean, clear plastic hose

PUT IT TOGETHER:

STEP 1: Fill one jug with tap water. Add several drops of food coloring.

STEP 2: Set this jug on a table or counter.

STEP 3: Set the other jug on the floor nearby.

STEP 4: Insert the hose into the top jug. Push it all the way in. Make sure its end is near the bottom of the jug.

STEP 5: Place the other end of the hose near the bottom jug. Include some loops in the hose.

STEP 6: Gently suck on the bottom end of the hose. As the water nears your mouth, quickly stick the end inside the bottom jug. What happens?

STEP 6

REUSABLE KNOWLEDGE:

Did you realize that the air around you is constantly pushing on you? This pressure is called atmospheric pressure. It's what makes a siphon work. Sucking air out of the tube decreases the pressure inside. This causes atmospheric pressure to push water into the tube. As the water moves through the tube, its pressure is lowered again. Atmospheric pressure keeps pushing until the jug is dry.

RECYCLING MILK JUGS

Milk jugs are recycled into soap bottles, garden products, and plastic lumber. 3D printers even use old milk jugs for printing material. Why not use old milk jugs to make more milk jugs? Used jugs could contain impurities, making them unsafe for food packaging.

CARTESIAN DIVER

Your command of this little diver will amaze you. You can thank the properties of gases for this experiment.

BRANCH OF SCIENCE: CHEMISTRY
CONCEPT: BOYLE'S LAW

YOU'LL NEED:

- Clean, empty 2-liter soda bottle with cap
- Ruler
- Water
- Small sauce packet

PUT IT TOGETHER:

STEP 1: Fill the bottle with water to within 2 inches (5 cm) of the top.

STEP 2: Drop a sauce packet into the bottle. Make sure it floats just below the water. Experiment with several packets until you find one that works.

STEP 3: Screw the cap on the bottle.

STEP 4: Squeeze the bottle. What happens?

STEP 5: Let it go. What happens now?

REUSABLE KNOWLEDGE:

An air pocket inside the packet keeps it light enough to float. When you squeeze the bottle, the air pocket becomes smaller. Now the "diver" sinks. This marvel is explained by Boyle's Law. Boyle's Law states that increasing pressure will decrease volume and vice versa.

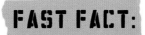

FAST FACT:

Water is very heavy. It weighs 64 pounds per cubic foot (1,025 kilograms per cubic meter). The deeper a diver goes under water, the more pressure he or she feels. Deep-water divers cannot breathe because of the pressure on their lungs. Pressurized air from a SCUBA tank gives lungs enough pressure to combat water pressure. SCUBA stands for Self-Contained Underwater Breathing Apparatus.

UPSIDE DOWN WATER

Water can easily flow through a window screen, right? Not so fast! In this experiment water does the unthinkable.

BRANCH OF SCIENCE: CHEMISTRY
CONCEPT: SURFACE TENSION

YOU'LL NEED:

- Clean, empty milk jug
- Water
- 6-inch (15-cm) square of vinyl window screen
- Rubber band
- Several toothpicks
- A friend

PUT IT TOGETHER:

STEP 1: Fill the jug about 1/3 full of water.

STEP 2: Place the screen over the opening in the jug. Wrap the rubber band around the screen to hold it to the neck of the milk jug.

STEP 3: Outside or over a sink, carefully turn the jug upside down. Hold on to the jug's handle.

STEP 4: Steady the jug while holding the handle. Make sure not to squeeze it. What happens?

STEP 5: Have a friend carefully push a toothpick through a hole in the screen. What happens?

STEP 2

REUSABLE KNOWLEDGE:

Water molecules are strongly attracted to one another. This attraction is called cohesion. Under the water's surface, molecules are attracted equally in all directions. But this attraction is unequal at the water's surface. Here water molecules are attracted inward only. So molecules act like a thin elastic skin where they meet air. We call this surface tension. This skin stretches across the screen holes. It holds water inside the jug.

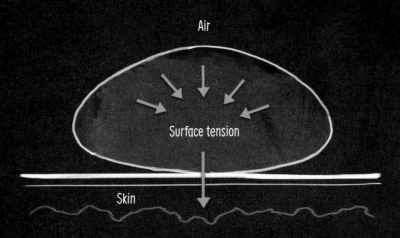

Air

Surface tension

Skin

A WATERY SKIN

Surface tension acts like a skin on water's surface. Small drops of liquid are spherical because cohesion pulls the molecules inward.

BALLOON INFLATOR

Blowing up balloons can wear out your lungs.
Let something else do the work. A little
chemical reaction is all it takes.

BRANCH OF SCIENCE: CHEMISTRY
CONCEPT: ACID/BASE REACTION

YOU'LL NEED:

- Balloon (not inflated)
- Funnel
- 1/8 cup (38 grams) baking soda
- Clean, empty pop bottle, 20 ounces
  (0.6 liter) or smaller
- Vinegar

PUT IT TOGETHER:

STEP 1: Place the tip of the funnel inside the balloon.

STEP 2: Pour the baking soda into the funnel. Shake the baking soda into the balloon.

STEP 3: Fill the bottle about half full of vinegar.

STEP 4: Remove the funnel. Stretch the neck of the balloon over the top of the bottle. Make sure none of the baking soda falls into the vinegar.

STEP 5: Hold the neck of the balloon tightly to the bottle. Tip the balloon to dump the baking soda into the vinegar. What happens?

STEP 1

STEP 4

REUSABLE KNOWLEDGE:

Vinegar is an acid, and baking soda is a base. Acids and bases react to make a new product. In this case, carbon dioxide gas is made. You can't always see a gas, but in this experiment the gas is easy to detect. It expands to fill the balloon. If you've ever made a cake, you've seen an acid and base reaction. Bubbles from reacting ingredients make the cake light and fluffy.

RECYCLING SODA BOTTLES

Think you'd look good wearing pop bottles? How about using them to decorate your home? That's exactly where most recycled PET ends up. It is processed into many new materials including carpet fiber, T-shirt fabric, shoes, and luggage. It is also used to make new PET containers for food and nonfood products.

VINEGAR ROCKET

A blasting rocket is an exciting experiment. This rocket uses things you find around your house. It packs a punch and explains an important physics law.

YOU'LL NEED:

- Clean, empty drink bottle
- Vinegar
- 1 teaspoon of baking soda
- 1 square of toilet tissue
- Tape
- Cardboard oatmeal or cornmeal canister (must be wide enough for the pop bottle to fit into)
- Cork that fits snugly in the mouth of the pop bottle

BRANCH OF SCIENCE: PHYSICS
CONCEPT: NEWTON'S THIRD LAW OF MOTION

PUT IT TOGETHER:

STEP 1: Fill the bottle about 1/3 full of vinegar. Set it aside.

STEP 2: Place the baking soda in the center of the toilet tissue. Carefully roll the tissue into a tight tube around the baking soda.

STEP 3: Fold the ends over, and tape them in place to make a small packet. Make sure the packet is small enough to fit inside the mouth of the pop bottle.

STEP 4: Find an open area outside. Place the cardboard canister on the ground or prop it at an angle with bricks or rocks. Make sure the canister is not pointing toward people, animals, or windows.

STEP 5: Drop the packet into the bottle. Quickly cork it. Put the bottle cork side down inside the canister.

STEP 6: Back several yards (meters) away, and wait. It may take a little while for the rocket to take off. Do not go near it as you wait!

STEP 7: Search out the landing place of your rocket. Then do the experiment again!

STEP 3

STEP 5

REUSABLE KNOWLEDGE:

This experiment shows Newton's Third Law of Motion. This law states that for every action there is an equal and opposite reaction. The vinegar and baking soda reaction forms carbon dioxide. The carbon dioxide explodes backward from the bottle. An equal force pushes the bottle forward. This is the same principle that lifts rockets into space.

SUB IRRIGATED PLANTER

Do you like gardening? Are you sometimes afraid of watering your plants too little or too much? Try this project. It uses an important biology concept to keep plants watered just right.

BRANCH OF SCIENCE: BIOLOGY
CONCEPT: CAPILLARY ACTION

YOU'LL NEED:

- Clean, empty 2-liter bottle
- Ruler
- Marker
- Utility knife
- 3 strips of cotton from an old T-shirt,
  1 inch wide x 4 inches long (2.5 cm x 10 cm)
- 3 cups (700 g) potting soil
- Lettuce or herb seeds
- Water

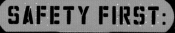

SAFETY FIRST:

Have an adult help when using sharp tools such as a utility knife.

STEP 1: Make a mark 3 inches (8 cm) from the top of the bottle. Use the utility knife to cut a small "x" at this spot.

STEP 2: Repeat Step 1 to make a total of six small x's. Make them evenly spaced around the bottle 3 inches (8 cm) from the top. This will allow air to reach the soil.

STEP 3: Use the utility knife to cut off the top half of the bottle.

STEP 4: Turn the top upside down, and place it inside the bottom half.

STEP 5: Push the fabric strips through the neck of the bottle. They should extend through the neck and touch the bottle's bottom.

STEP 6: Pack the soil in around the cotton strips.

STEP 3

STEP 5

STEP 7: Plant seeds in the soil according to the package directions. Lightly water the seeds from the top.

STEP 8: Lift the top, and pour several inches of water into the bottle bottom. Replace the top.

STEP 9: Wait for your seeds to sprout and grow. Refill the bottom with water as needed. The water in the bottom of the bottle will keep your plants watered.

REUSABLE KNOWLEDGE:

Like a straw, plant cells draw water and minerals upward. This upward flow is called capillary action. Your waterer also uses capillary action. Water moves through openings in the cotton and soil to reach the plant's roots.

LAVA LAMP

A lava lamp gives off a one-of-a-kind glow. Its dancing blobs bring hours of enjoyment. Make your own with this project. Then pride yourself on knowing the science behind it.

BRANCH OF SCIENCE: CHEMISTRY
CONCEPT: OIL AND WATER IMMISCIBILITY

YOU'LL NEED:

- Clean soda or water bottle (any size)
- Water
- Vegetable oil
- Food coloring (any color)
- Effervescent tablets (Alka-Seltzer)
- Battery-operated tea light

PUT IT TOGETHER:

STEP 1: Fill the bottle about ¼ full of water.

STEP 2: Pour vegetable oil into the bottle until it is nearly full.

STEP 3: Add 6 to 10 drops of food coloring into the bottle. Shake the bottle if needed to dissolve the food coloring.

STEP 4: Wait until the water and oil have separated. Place ¼ of an effervescent tablet into the bottle. Watch the show!

STEP 5: When the bubbles stop, place another ¼ tablet into the bottle. This time place the lit tea light upside down in the top of the bottle.

STEP 6: Take the lamp into a dark room for a lava lamp experience.

STEP 7: Add more tablets, ¼ at a time, to keep the fun going.

STEP 4

REUSABLE KNOWLEDGE:

The oil and water don't mix together. Why? Water is much denser than oil. Its molecules are more tightly packed together than oil's are. This makes water sink. The structure of the molecules is different for oil and water too. Water's molecules are polar, meaning they have a negative charge on one end and a positive charge on the other. Their charges hold the molecules to each other. Oil is nonpolar, without a charge, and doesn't mingle with the water molecules. The fizzing tablet releases gas. As the gas rises to the surface, it pulls colored water with it. After the gas escapes, the water blobs sink back to the bottom of the bottle.

COMPOSTING WORM FARM

Recycle more than a pop bottle with this project.
Recycle your kitchen scraps too. This project
does more than keep garbage out of a landfill.
It improves the environment!

BRANCH OF SCIENCE: **BIOLOGY**
CONCEPT: **SOIL SCIENCE**

YOU'LL NEED:

- Clean, empty 2-liter bottle
- Utility knife
- 16.9-ounce (0.5-liter) water bottle
  filled with room temperature water
- Small scoop
- Ruler
- Sand
- Soil
- Fruit and vegetable peels
- 1/2 cup (0.12 l) water
- 3 or 4 earthworms

SAFETY FIRST:

Have an adult help when using sharp tools such as a utility knife.

PUT IT TOGETHER:

STEP 1: Use the utility knife to cut the top off the 2-liter bottle. Cut it where the bottle starts to get narrow near the top. Discard the top.

STEP 2: Center the water bottle inside the 2-liter bottle. This will keep the worms near the outside of the bottle so you can watch them.

STEP 3: Carefully scoop about 1 inch (2.5 cm) of sand into the larger bottle. Make sure the water bottle stays in place.

STEP 4: Add about 1 inch (2.5 cm) of soil.

STEP 5: Add a layer of fruit and vegetable peels.

STEP 6: Continue layering 1-inch (2.5-cm) layers of sand, soil, and scraps. Stop when you reach about 2 inches (5 cm) from the top of the bottle.

STEP 2

STEP 5

STEP 7: Slowly pour water over the layers to make them slightly damp.

STEP 8: Add the worms.

STEP 9: Place the bottle in a cool, dark place.

STEP 10: Add small amounts of water every couple days to keep the worm farm moist. Watch daily until the worms have composted all the scraps.

STEP 11: After several weeks, pour the newly composted soil and worms into a planter or garden. Let them continue their work.

REUSABLE KNOWLEDGE:

Worms are nature's great recyclers. Worms turn food scraps and dead plants into rich soil fertilizer. As worms eat, their bodies change scraps into compost. They poop out this fertilizer to keep plants strong and healthy. Test it out yourself. Do plants grow better in composted soil or regular soil?

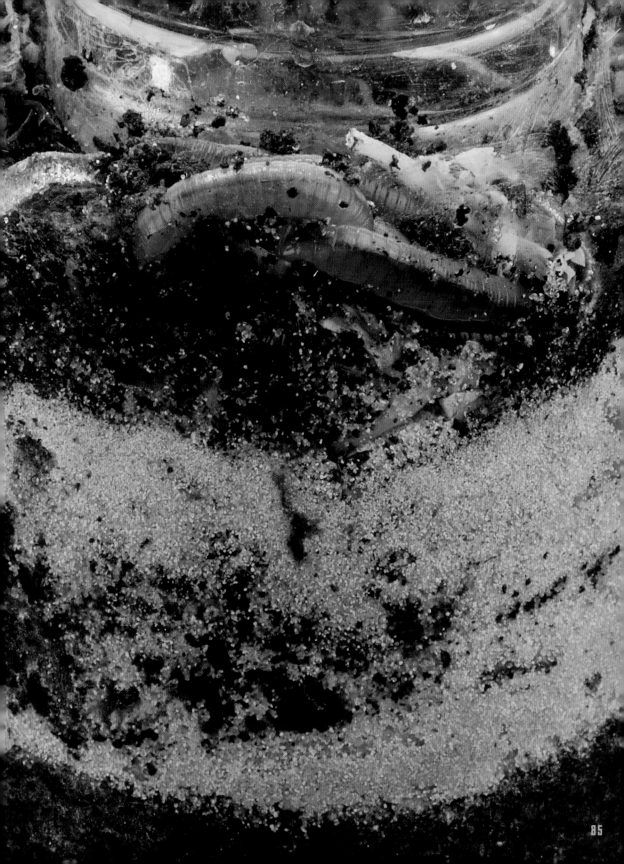

CHAPTER FOUR

AMAZING CARDBOARD TUBE SCIENCE

GET ROLLING!

Don't throw away that empty toilet paper roll! You have valuable scientific equipment in your hand! Why not try your hand at being a paper-tube engineer?

Like any engineer, you'll need to keep a few things in mind as you work. Sometimes, the first time you try a project, it doesn't work. Don't give up! Check over each part of your work to see if you can fix it. If you don't have all of the materials that a project requires, don't let that stop you either. See if you can redesign the project with materials you do have. And of course, follow all safety guidelines, and grab a grownup when you need one.

What are you waiting for? It's time to get rolling!

ABOUT CARDBOARD TUBES

This chapter divides cardboard tubes into long tubes and short tubes. Long tubes can come from a paper towel roll, a plastic wrap or aluminum foil container, or a wrapping paper tube that you have cut into pieces. Short tubes come from toilet paper rolls or long tubes that you have cut to about that size.

KAZOO

Place your hand on your throat and hum. Do you feel vibrations? Vibrations are the basis of sound. With this kazoo, you can enhance your humming vibrations and create a musical buzz.

SCIENCE BRANCH: **PHYSICS**
CONCEPT: **ACOUSTICS**

YOU'LL NEED:

- Long tube
- Ruler
- Scissors
- Rubber band
- Waxed paper or plastic grocery bag
- Sharp pencil

PUT IT TOGETHER:

STEP 1: Cut a 6-inch (15-cm) piece from a long tube.

STEP 2: Cut a circle about the size of a dessert plate from the waxed paper or plastic bag.

STEP 3: Cover one end of your tube with the waxed paper or plastic bag. Use the rubber band to hold it in place.

STEP 4: Use the sharp pencil to punch a hole in the middle of the top side of your tube.

STEP 5: Place the open end of the tube to your mouth. Hum or sing using the sound "ta ta ta." Experiment with high and low pitches.

REUSABLE KNOWLEDGE:

When you talk or sing, vibrations start in your larynx, which houses your vocal cords. The vibrations move into other parts of your throat and head. The vibrating body parts bump into air molecules. That starts the air molecules vibrating. When the vibrating air hits a person's eardrum, he or she hears your sound. Short, quick vibrations make a high pitch. Longer, slower vibrations make a low pitch.

With this kazoo, you send your vibrations through the air to the piece of waxed paper or grocery bag. The air causes the paper or bag to vibrate. But it vibrates at a slightly different speed than your vocal cords. So the kazoo produces a sound that is similar, but not identical, to your hum.

HOLE IN YOUR HAND

Your eyes and brain are usually pretty good partners. Your eyes collect light that reflects from the objects in front of you. They send the information to the brain for processing. The brain uses that information to recognize what you are seeing. With just a tube and your hand, however, you can get your eyes to send a message that will really confuse your brain.

SCIENCE BRANCH: **ANATOMY AND PHYSIOLOGY**
CONCEPT: **OPTICAL ILLUSIONS**

YOU'LL NEED:

- – Paper towel tube
- – Your hand

PUT IT TOGETHER:

STEP 1: With one hand, hold the paper towel tube up to your eye. Look through the tube as if you were looking through a telescope.

STEP 2: Hold the other hand up next to the tube, resting the side of your hand against the tube.

STEP 3: Stare straight ahead, and notice what you see. Make sure both eyes are open.

REUSABLE KNOWLEDGE:

Since your eyes are located about 2 inches (5 cm) apart, each one captures a slightly different image. Your brain overlaps the information from each eye to figure out what you are seeing. Usually your eyes see the same scene from a slightly different angle. Overlapping the two images gives you depth perception, or the ability to figure out how far away something is. In this activity, your brain follows its usual system of overlapping the two images, but they are of two different things. So you end up seeing a hole in your hand!

ARE YOU RIGHT-EYED OR LEFT-EYED?

It is not just right-handedness and left-handedness that makes us different. You can also be right-eyed or left-eyed. Use a long tube to figure out which eye is dominant, and shed some light on a mystery that has baffled scientists.

SCIENCE BRANCH: ANATOMY AND PHYSIOLOGY
CONCEPT: VISION

YOU'LL NEED:

- Long tube
- Wall with a light switch

PUT IT TOGETHER:

STEP 1: Grab a paper towel tube with both hands. Hold it in front of you with your arms stretched out.

STEP 2: Point the tube at a light switch or other small object on the wall. Back up until you can see the entire switch through the tube.

STEP 3: With your arms still extended, focus on the light switch. Without moving your body, close your left eye. Can you see the light switch through the tube?

STEP 4: Close your right eye, and open the left. Can you see the light switch now?

REUSABLE KNOWLEDGE:

Most people will hold the tube so that they see the light switch with only one eye. By closing one eye at a time, you can see which eye is lined up to view the switch. That is your dominant eye. As you saw in Hole in Your Hand (p. 90), both eyes send an image to your brain. Your brain usually combines the images. Sometimes, however, our brains pick the image from one eye over the image from the other. Scientists aren't sure why.

MARSHMALLOW SHOOTER

Squeeze your arm muscles tight. Your muscles are full of energy. With this shooter, you can transfer some of that energy to a marshmallow and send it flying across the room. Ready. Aim. Fire!

SCIENCE BRANCH: PHYSICS
CONCEPT: ENERGY TRANSFER AND STORAGE

YOU'LL NEED:

- 2 short tubes
- Ruler
- Pencil
- Scissors
- Masking tape
- Hole puncher
- 2 rubber bands
- Large marshmallows

PUT IT TOGETHER:

STEP 1: Use the pencil to draw a 3/4-inch (2-cm) line straight down from the opening of one of your tubes. Draw a second line about a finger's width away. Cut along the lines to make two slits.

STEP 2: Make a second, identical pair of slits directly opposite the opening from the first pair. This will be your outer tube. Set it aside.

STEP 3: Use the scissors to cut a straight line along the length of the other tube, leaving it shaped like a hot dog bun.

STEP 4: Roll this tube until it is about half its original width. Tape it firmly. This will be your inside tube.

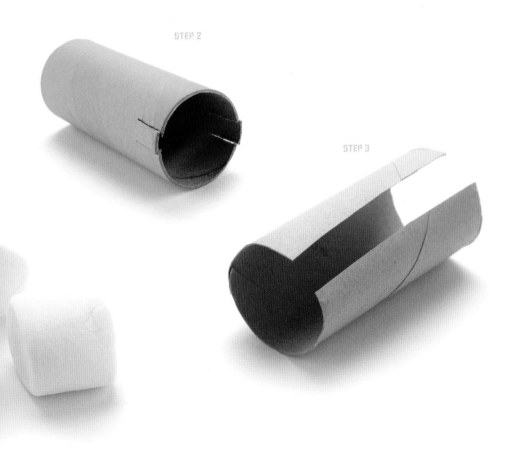

STEP 2

STEP 3

STEP 5: Punch a pair of holes in the inside tube to hold your pencil. Punch one hole about 1 inch (2.5 cm) from the top on one side. Punch another hole directly opposite from it. Slide the pencil through the hole to make a handle.

STEP 6: Slide the inside tube into the outer tube. Make sure that the slits on the outer tube point away from the pencil.

STEP 7: Slide a rubber band into the pair of slits on one side. Hook the rubber band around the pencil on the same side. Repeat with the second rubber band on the other side.

STEP 9: To fire your shooter, stick a large marshmallow into the firing end. Grab the outer tube with one hand. It's OK if your hands are on top of the rubber band. Pull the handle back, and fire away!

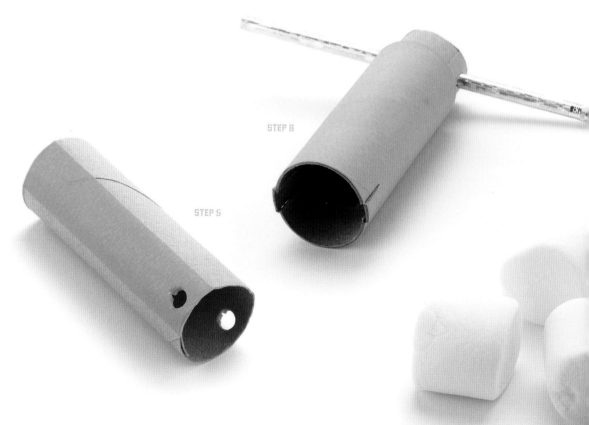

STEP 6

STEP 5

REUSABLE KNOWLEDGE:

When you use your shooter, you pass energy from your muscles to the rubber band to the marshmallow. You pull back the handle, and the rubber band stores some of the energy from your arm movement in its stretch. Scientists call this kind of stored energy potential energy because it has the potential to do work. Release the handle, and the rubber band springs into action. The stored energy becomes moving energy, called kinetic energy. The inside tube strikes the marshmallow, and it passes that kinetic energy on. Now the marshmallow has enough energy to fly across the room.

MARBLE RUN

Hold a marble in your hand, and it doesn't seem like it has energy. But drop it in a marble run, and it speeds off. It even has enough energy to run uphill! Start by building the pieces described in the following experiment. Then design your own energy-releasing raceway.

SCIENCE BRANCH: PHYSICS
CONCEPT: GRAVITATIONAL POTENTIAL ENERGY

YOU'LL NEED:

- Long and short tubes
- Ruler
- Scussirs
- Scrap paper
- Masking tape
- Pencil
- Paper plate
- Blue painter's tape
- Empty soda can
- Marbles

PUT IT TOGETHER:

STEP 1: First, create the pieces you will want to include in your design. To build a tunnel, cut a 1-inch (2.5-cm) U-shape out of the end of a tube so that a marble can drop in from above.

STEP 2: To create troughs, cut some of the tubes in half lengthwise. Each tube will give you two troughs.

STEP 3: To make an uphill bounce, take a trough made from a paper towel tube. Tape a piece of scrap paper to one end to form a wall. Arrange this piece so that the marble runs uphill, hits the wall, and heads back down.

STEP 4: To make a funnel, trace the bottom of a soda can in the center of a paper plate. Cut a straight line from the side of the plate to the circle you drew. Then cut out the circle. Hold the plate on either side of the straight cut. Overlap the sides to make a funnel. Tape the plate together in this position. Tape a tunnel to the bottom of the funnel to direct the marble into the next piece of your run.

TIP:

Painter's tape is designed to be removed from walls without tearing paint or wallpaper. Even with painter's tape, though, you should test it out before taping the whole run. Stick a piece of tape on an area that is not obvious. Then remove it to make sure that it will not mark up your wall.

STEP 1

STEP 2

STEP 5: Before you start to build your marble run, ask for permission to tape it to a wall or door using blue painter's tape.

STEP 6: Place the pieces you made in any order you like. As you add each piece, test your run. If the marble pops out of the track before it gets to the end, it is moving too fast. Slow it down by adding an uphill bounce or making the marble move in a straight line for a segment. You can also use tape to create walls or ceilings at places where the marble pops out.

STEP 7: Place the empty soda can upside down underneath the final part of your run to serve as an ending bell.

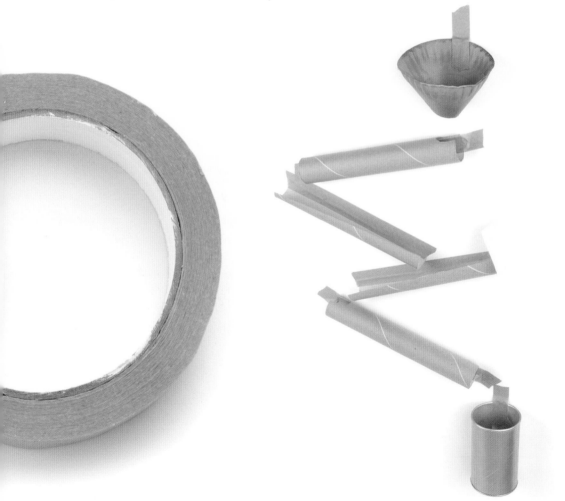

REUSABLE KNOWLEDGE:

A marble held up high has more energy than a marble sitting on the floor. How? You give it energy by lifting it up, against the force of gravity. Energy cannot be created or destroyed. It only moves from one object to another. The energy from your arm is transferred to the marble as potential energy. When you release the marble, gravity pulls it down. The potential energy turns into kinetic energy, just as it does with the marshmallow shooter. The higher you lift the marble, the more potential energy it has. As you can see with your uphill bounce piece, the marble even has enough energy to run uphill.

ON A ROLL

When you inflate a balloon, you use energy to stretch the rubber so it holds more air. The stretched rubber stores that energy, ready to force the air out as soon as it has a chance. Put your balloon's energy to work driving this recycled racecar.

SCIENCE BRANCH: PHYSICS
CONCEPT: NEWTON'S 2ND LAW OF MOTION

YOU'LL NEED:

- Wooden skewer
- Ruler
- Scissors
- 2 large marshmallows
- 2 pairs of matching bottle caps
- Short paper tube
- 2 straws
- Tape
- Balloon

PUT IT TOGETHER:

STEP 1: Have an adult help you to cut two 4-inch (10-cm) lengths from the wooden skewer for axles.

STEP 2: Cut a large marshmallow in half. Press each half into one of your bottle caps, sticky side down. Repeat for the other two wheels.

STEP 3: Connect one set of wheels by sticking a skewer into the center of the marshmallows. Repeat for the other set.

STEP 4: Cut a square hole, about 1 1/2 inches (4 cm) wide, in the top of your paper tube.

STEP 5: Cut a straw into two 2-inch (5-cm) long pieces. These will hold the axles and wheels.

STEP 6: Flip the tube so that the square hole is facing down. Tape the pieces of straw across the bottom of the tube so that the wheels will stick off the side of the car. Make sure the straws are exactly parallel.

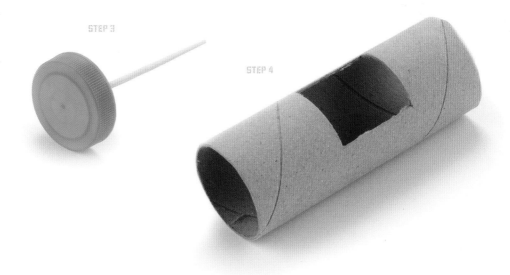

STEP 3

STEP 4

STEP 7: Attach the front wheels by removing one bottle cap from its skewer, sticking the skewer through the straw, and reattaching the wheel on the other side. Repeat for the back wheels.

STEP 8: Insert the second straw into the mouth of the balloon. Twist the balloon tightly, and tape it to the straw. Air should only be able to enter and leave the balloon through the straw.

STEP 9: Insert the straw into the square hole, and tape it so that end of the straw sticks straight out of the back of the car.

STEP 10: To make the car move, blow into the straw to inflate the balloon. Squeeze the end of the straw to hold the air in while you set the car on the ground and arrange the wheels.

STEP 11: Release your grip, and the car should roll across the ground.

REUSABLE KNOWLEDGE:

In the 1600s a scientist named Isaac Newton said that for every action there is an equal and opposite reaction. When you release the balloon, the stretched rubber pushes the air out. At the same time, the air pushes back against the balloon with an equal force. Since the balloon is attached to your car, the air pushes the car forward. This is the same principle that allows rockets to take off. A rocket engine pushes hot gases down. At the same time, those gases push back against the rocket and lift it into space.

FLASHLIGHT

Like everything else in the universe, metal wires are made up of atoms. Atoms are made of particles called electrons, protons, and neutrons. If you get the electrons in atoms moving, you've got electricity. In this activity, you will build a circuit to move electrons and light up a flashlight.

SCIENCE BRANCH: PHYSICS
CONCEPT: ELECTRICAL CIRCUITS

YOU'LL NEED:

- An adult to help you
- Old string of holiday lights with the plug removed
- Ruler
- Wire cutter and stripper
- 2 "C"-sized batteries
- Masking tape or electrical tape
- Long tube
- Hole punch
- 2 brads, thin wire nails with small longish but rounded heads
- Paper clip

PUT IT TOGETHER:

STEP 1: Have an adult use the wire cutters to cut one bulb from the string of holiday lights. Leave as much wire as possible on either side of the bulb.

STEP 2: Have an adult strip about 1 inch (2.5 cm) of plastic coating from the wire on one end of the bulb. Repeat for the other side of the wire.

STEP 3: There will be at least one long wire in the light set that does not connect to the bulbs. Have an adult use wire cutters to cut three lengths from this wire, each about 8 inches (20 cm) long. Have the adult strip 1 inch (2.5 cm) of coating from both ends of each wire. These will be your long wires.

STEP 4: Test your lightbulb. Touch the two wires attached to the bulb to either side of one of your batteries. If you are using LED bulbs, electricity can only flow one way through them, so you may have to try reversing which side of the battery meets which wire. The bulb should light up. If you cannot get it to light up, repeat Step 1 to find a working bulb.

STEP 2

STEP 3

STEP 4

TIP:

Most holiday lights will fit into the wire stripper slots for 20 or 22 AWG.

STEP 5: Lay out your batteries so that the positive terminal (the bump) on one end meets the negative terminal (the flat end) of the other. Tape the batteries firmly, making sure the ends stay pressed together. This is your battery pack. Test your bulb against the two exposed sides. If it does not light, tape the batteries more tightly.

STEP 6: Take one of your long wires and attach it to one end of your bulb by twisting the exposed metal ends together. Secure the connection by taping it with masking tape or electrical tape. Repeat, adding another long wire to the other side of your lightbulb. Once again, touch the wires to the battery pack to make sure your connections are good.

STEP 7: Punch a hole about 1/2 inch (1.3 cm) from the end of your tube. Punch another hole opposite the first. Thread the wires on either side of the light bulb through the holes so that the bulb is centered at the end of your tube.

STEP 8: On the opposite end of the flashlight, punch one hole about 1 inch (2.5 cm) from the end. Measure 1 inch (2.5 cm) from the first hole, and punch a second hole. To make this punch, you will need to squeeze the side of the tube to make a fold, and then punch half a circle into the fold.

STEP 9: Wrap the exposed wire from one side of your bulb around the top of a brad. Insert the brad into one of holes. Reach inside the tube, and open the legs of the brad so it stays in place.

TIP:

The sturdier the tube, the better. Cardboard tubes from inside aluminum foil and waxed paper are often stronger than those from paper towels.

STEP 5

STEP 10: Take the long wire that you have not yet used. Wrap one end around the second brad. Slip the paper clip onto the brad, and insert the brad into the second hole. Open the legs of the brad to hold it in place.

STEP 11: Tape the wire coming from the brad to the center of one terminal on your battery pack. Tape the remaining wire from the lightbulb to the center of the other terminal of your battery pack.

STEP 12: To turn the flashlight on, twist the paper clip so it touches both brads. To turn the flashlight off, twist the paperclip so that it does not touch the second brad.

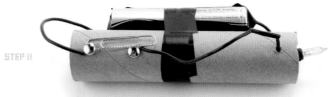

STEP 11

REUSABLE KNOWLEDGE:

Electrons move from areas with a negative charge to areas with a positive charge. Each battery has a negative end and a positive end. When you connect batteries with wires, electrons move from one side to the other. Stick a lightbulb along that path, and the electrons will light it up as they move. This is called an electric circuit.

It's no accident that the word circuit sounds like circle. To keep the electrons moving, you need a complete circle from one battery terminal to the other. If you twist the paper clip so that the wires are no longer connected, you create an opening in the path. Electricity cannot flow. This is called an open circuit. To get electricity moving again, you must connect the paperclip and close the circuit. Then the bulb lights up.

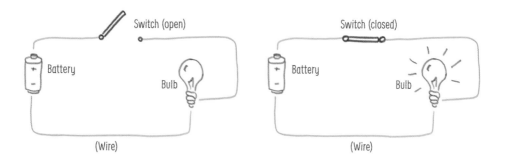

PLANTABLE PLANTER

Inside a tiny grass seed is a plant embryo and a store of food to help it grow. When the seed is soaked in water, that's the new plant's cue to press its way out and sprout. Use a short tube to create a cute container for your sprouting seeds, and then plant them—tube and all—in your yard.

SCIENCE BRANCH: BIOLOGY
CONCEPT: SEEDS AND SPROUTS

YOU'LL NEED:

- Ruler
- Short tube
- Scissors
- Felt-tipped pens
- 3/4 cup (177 grams) of potting soil
- 1 teaspoon of grass seed
- Water

PUT IT TOGETHER:

STEP 1: Draw four 1-inch (2.5-cm) lines at equal distances around one end of your tube. Cut along each line to make four small flaps.

STEP 2: Fold the flaps so that each flap overlaps the one before it. Tuck one side of the last flap under the first flap. Press the flaps tightly to make a flat bottom for your planter.

STEP 3: Using the felt-tipped pens, draw a face on the planter.

STEP 4: Fill the planter 3/4 full of potting soil. Spread the seeds on top of the soil. Add a thin layer of soil to cover the seeds.

STEP 5: Water the seeds, but be careful not to add so much water that the roll is drenched.

STEP 6: Place your planter in a warm place. Keep the soil moist but not soaked. Your seeds should sprout hair in 5 to 14 days.

STEP 7: Plant your sprouts, tube and all, in a bald spot in your lawn.

STEP 4

STEP 2

TIP:
Set your planter on a plate to catch any dirty water that might leak from the bottom.

REUSABLE KNOWLEDGE:

Even inside a seed, the embryo has a top and a bottom. One end is set to become roots. The other will become a stem. But you don't have to worry about planting your seeds upside down. Plants sense gravity. Roots and stems will turn to grow in the right direction. A bonus to starting seed in this planter is that it will break down in the ground and become soil. You won't even have to disturb your sprouts to move them to your lawn.

Capstone Young Readers
1710 Roe Crest Drive, North Mankato, Minnesota 56003
www.mycapstone.com

Library of Congress Cataloging-in-Publication Data
Names: Enz, Tammy, author. | Wheeler-Toppen, Jodi, author.
Title: Recycled science : bring out your science genius with
soda bottles, potato chip bags, and more unexpected stuff / by Tammy Enz
and Jodi Wheeler-Toppen.
Description: North Mankato, Minnesota : Capstone Press, [2017] | Series:
Recycled science | Compilation of four separately published books. |
Audience: Ages 9-15.? | Audience: Grades 4 to 6.? | Includes
bibliographical references and index.
Identifiers: LCCN 2015045605|
ISBN 9781623706975 (paperback) |
ISBN 9781623706982 (eBook PDF)
Subjects: LCSH: Handicraft—Juvenile literature. | Science—Study and teaching—Juvenile
literature. | Recycling (Waste, etc.)—Juvenile literature.
Classification: LCC TT160 .E59 2017 | DDC 745.5—dc23
LC record available at http://lccn.loc.gov/2015045605

Editorial Credits
Brenda Haugen, editor; Russell Griesmer, designer; Tracey Cummins, media specialist;
Kathy McColley, production specialist

Photo Credits
Capstone Studio: Karon Dubke (All images except the following); Shutterstock: Georgios Kollidas, 23,
105, JIPEN, 51, silver tiger, 55

Design elements provided by Shutterstock: bimka, FINDEEP, fourb, Golbay, jannoon028, mexrix,
Picsfive, Sarunyu_foto, STILLFX, Your Design